NO LONGER PROPERTY
OF ANYTHINK
RANGEVIEW LIBRARY
DISTRICT

anythink

spot

PETS

TURTLES

by Mari Schuh

AMICUS | AMICUS INK

heat lamp

eyes

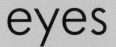

Look for these words and pictures as you read.

shell

beak

A turtle swims in its tank.

See it go!

Turtles are reptiles.
A reptile has scales.

heat lamp

Do you see the heat lamp?
It gives off light and heat.
Turtles need to stay warm.

eyes

Do you see its eyes?
They are wide open.
Turtles can see very well.

Do you see its hard shell?
It is made of bone.
It covers the turtle's soft body.

shell

beak

Do you see its beak?
Turtles have no teeth.
They eat pellets and leaves.

A box turtle hides in its shell.
What will it do next?

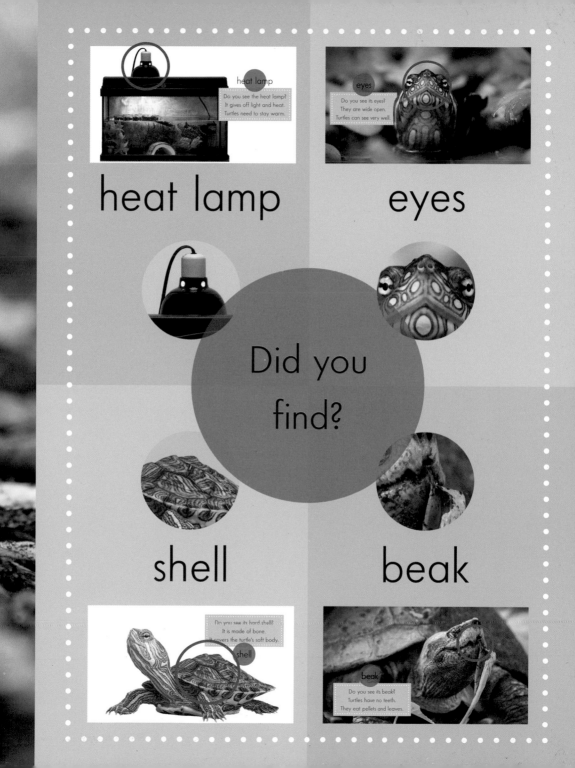

heat lamp

Do you see the heat lamp?
It gives off light and heat.
Turtles need to stay warm.

eyes

Do you see its eyes?
They are wide open.
Turtles can see very well.

Did you find?

shell

beak

Do you see its hard shell?
It is made of bone.
It covers the turtle's soft body.

shell

beak

Do you see its beak?
Turtles have no teeth.
They eat pellets and leaves.

spot

Spot is published by Amicus and Amicus Ink
P.O. Box 1329, Mankato, MN 56002
www.amicuspublishing.us

Copyright © 2019 Amicus.
International copyright reserved in all countries.
No part of this book may be reproduced in any form
without written permission from the publisher.

Library of Congress Cataloging-in-Publication Data
Names: Schuh, Mari C., 1975- author.
Title: Turtles / by Mari Schuh.
Description: Mankato, Minnesota : Amicus/Amicus Ink,
  [2019] | Series: Spot. Pets | Audience: K to grade 3.
Identifiers: LCCN 2017038877 (print) | LCCN 2017048186
  (ebook) | ISBN 9781681514536 (pdf) | ISBN
  9781681513713 (library bound) | ISBN 9781681522913
Subjects: LCSH: Turtles as pets--Juvenile literature. | Turtles-
  Juvenile literature.
Classification: LCC SF459.T8 (ebook) | LCC SF459.T8 S38
  2019 (print) | DDC 639.3/92--dc23
LC record available at https://lccn.loc.gov/2017038877

Printed in China

HC 10 9 8 7 6 5 4 3 2 1
PB 10 9 8 7 6 5 4 3 2 1

In memory of Charlie and Scooter —MS

Wendy Dieker, editor
Deb Miner, series designer
Ciara Beitlich, book designer
Holly Young, photo researcher

Photos by Alamy 10-11, 12-13; iStock
cover, 1, 14-15; Shutterstock 3, 4-5, 8-9;
ZooMed 6-7

TURTLES